Printed and Published in Great Britain by

C. THOMSON & CO., LTD., 185   Fleet Street, London, EC4A 2HS. © D. C. THOMSON & CO., LTD., 1981.
ISBN 0 85116 201 0

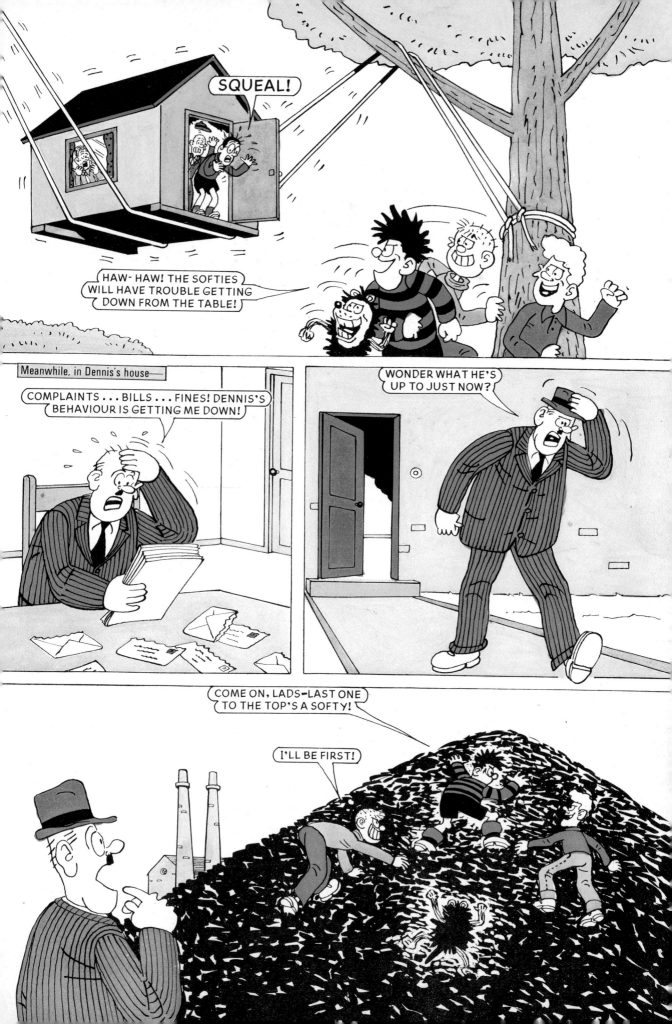

Coke joke!

Whack attack!

Disguise surprise!

For goodness sake—another fake!

Soon—

DOGGIE DEVICES

Piggy Bank

An extraordinary cash and carry!

Clock shock!

Presently—

AT LEAST TEACHER'S NEW EASY CHAIR'S HELPED US!

ZZZ!

IT'S SO COMFORTABLE THAT HE'S FALLEN ASLEEP!

GRUNT! SNORE!

WHISPER!—LET'S SNEAK OUT!

WHAT DID YOU SAY?

I SAID, LET'S SNEAK OUT!

STILL CAN'T HEAR YOU!

New cane—same old pain!

What a to-do with Elmer's lasso!

What a to-do with Elmer's lasso!

When Indians roam, Elmer goes home!

ROGER
GREAT BOOK! I'M NEARLY FINISHED!
The MASKED RAIDER STRIKES AGAIN
RRING!
WONDER WHO'S AT THE DOOR?
the Dodger

See Dad rage at the missing page!

Below you'll see Roger earning 10p!

MY JERSEY'S GOING TO LOOK DAFT!

DON'T PANIC, MUM— I'VE FOUND IT!

GREAT! HAVE 10p, ROGER!

And—

THE "LAST PAGE" DODGE IS WORKING WELL!

Then—

I'VE FOUND OUT ABOUT ROGER'S LATEST DODGE, MUM!

ULP! MUST CONSULT MY DODGE BOOKS!

PUP PARADE

CHRISTMAS EVE —

Hope we get a white Christmas, Sniffy!

Me, too, Bones!

DAFT PUP

What IS a white Christmas, Bones?

It's when you get deep snow at this time of year!

No snow!

AND—

White fright!

Zoom-zoom round the room!

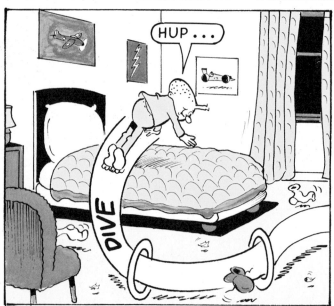

Crab grab!

DOGGIE DEVICES

Cat Punch Bag

Biffo's indeed working at speed!

The NIBBLERS

SCRITCH   SCRATCH   GORDONZOLA   HIS NIBS   CHEDDAR GEORGE   SNIFFLER   ENOR MOUSE   CHISELLER

WHICH ONE OF THE NIBBLERS HAS WON THE RACE TO THE LARDER? FOLLOW EACH MOUSE'S PATH IN TURN TO FIND OUT!

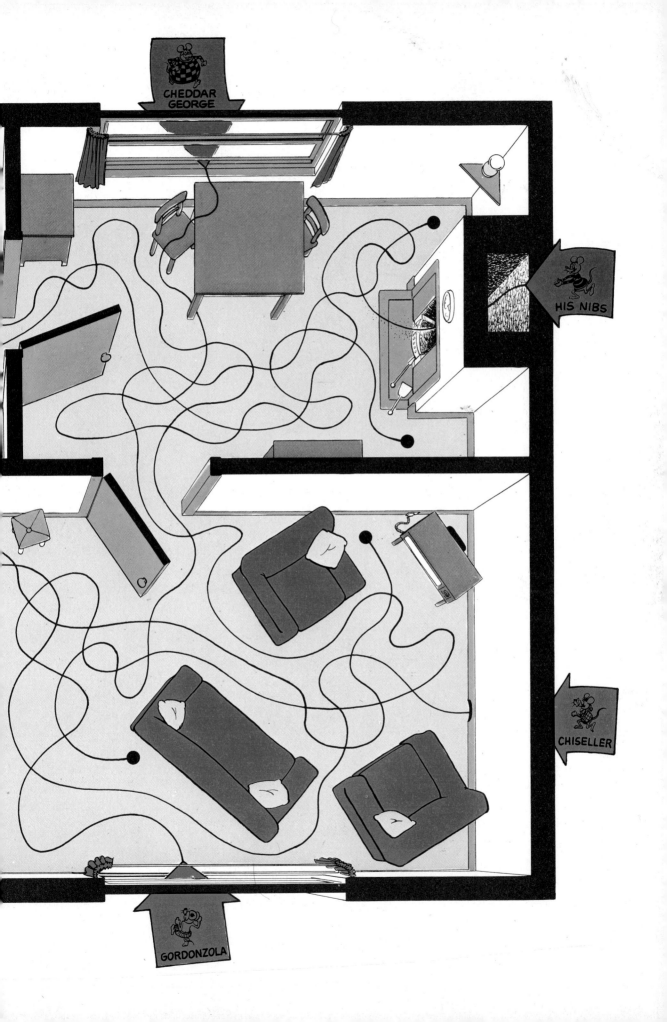

LITTLE PLUM

TRIBAL INSPECTION TODAY, AND ANY BRAVE WITH EVEN UM HAIR OUT OF PLACE GETS UM PESKY TASK TO DO!

PERFECT!

COMB

RUMBLE!

BETTER GET MYSELF BACK IN, QUICK!

WORM HOLE

IT'S UM DAILY BUFFALO STAMPEDE!

Getting trousers pressed in um wild west!

For the second half, his outfit's a laugh!

It's all go—clearing snow!

LOTS OF
MINNIE
the
MINX

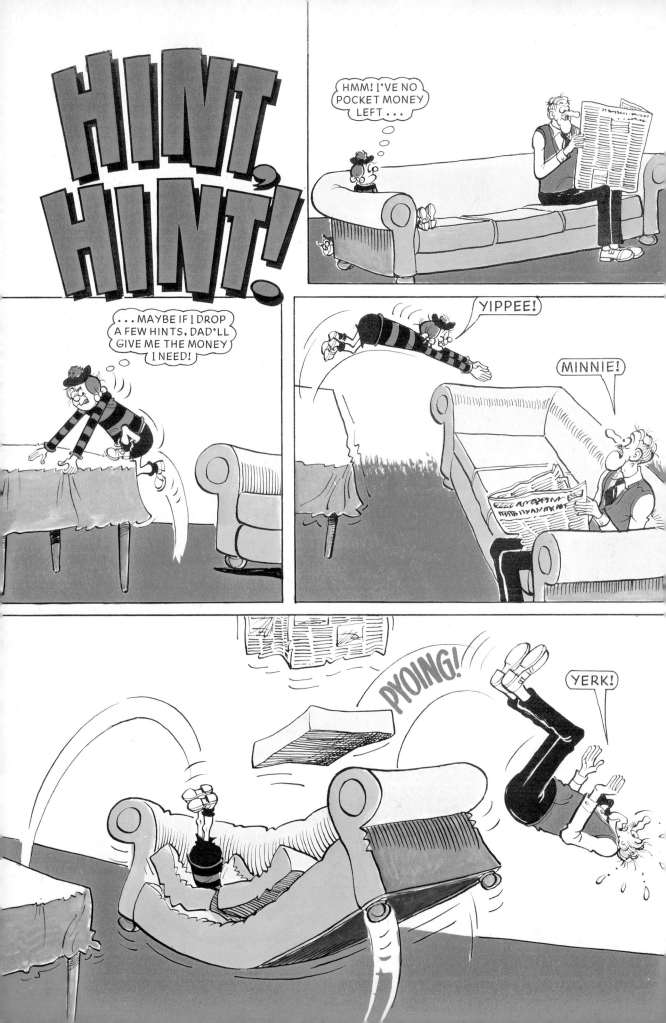

What a joke is Min's swimming stroke!

DINNER MONEY

POCKET MONEY

BUS MONEY

PRIZE MONEY

FOREIGN MONEY

TRANSFER MONEY

SAVINGS MONEY

HOLIDAY MONEY

CHOCOLATE MONEY

PAPER MONEY

Cash dash!

WELL, GIRL, HAVE YOU LEARNED ANYTHING ABOUT MONEY SINCE WE LAST SPOKE?

YES, I HAVE, DAD! THERE ARE LOTS OF KINDS OF MONEY...

...BUT THERE'S ONLY ONE KIND OF MINNIE, AND SHE'S OFF TO THE SWEET SHOP!

HEY, YOU MINX!

SWEETS

The weather forecast...

FUNNY SPELLS

Thunder wonder!

Now, at last, Dad's forecast!

DOGGIE DEVICES

Bunk Baskets

SMUDGE

My, my—a black eye!

MMM! LOOK AT THAT, FAMILY!

W- WHO A- ARE Y- YOU?

JUST CALL ME SOUPER- SAM!

TRY SOME SMELLY LAST MONTH'S SOUP, BEARS!

PONG! NIFF! SMELL! PHEW!

HEH! HEH! WHAT A SIGHT! HAR- HAR!

PEAS.

HANK, THE STOREKEEPER

NOW'S MY CHANCE!

Hill spill!

Good food!

Three bags full of Softy wool!

Smashed shell——foul smell!

Bad lad—Dad mad!

So—

OH, HE DID, DID HE?

Dennis's Dad has lost his lad, but he knows where to find him.

When he gets home, It's very well known, A slipper will strike from behind him!

TOM, DICK AND SALLY

Not funny—angry bunny!

Pen-pal for Sal!

Har! Har! Har! Funny old car!

Hard luck—cars stuck!

It's not wise to eat Rosie's pies!

LORD SNOOTY

At Bunkerton Castle—

LOOK WHAT I'VE MADE!

YUMMY!

WE'LL SAMPLE THEM FOR YOU, ROSIE!

HELP YOURSELVES!

But—

YEUGH!

GROO! HORRIBLE!

WELL, THOSE BIRDS LIKE THEM ANYWAY!

JUST THE JOB . . .

But—

...FOR BREAKING OPEN HARD NUTS! BOMBS AWAY!

GOOD SHOT, HENRY!

HO-HO!

CRACK!

THUD!

CRACK!

NUTS

Then—

I SAY, CAN I BUY SOME OF THOSE FOR MY PIE-EATING CONTEST?

WHY, OF COURSE!

PROUD

So—

READY, STEADY, GO!

BANG!

THIS SHOULD BE INTERESTING!

GRAND PIE EATING CONTEST

And—

UGH!

URK!

So—

HEH-HEH! HE'S A CASTOR OIL SALESMAN!

CASTOR OIL STAL

NEXT, PLEASE! CHUCKLE!

GROAN!

ACHE

SORE

Well, well—pies sell!

GNASHER'S TALE

BRRR!

CHATTER.

I WAS ALWAYS COLD IN MY KENNEL IN WINTER!

CHATTER! BRRRRR!

LIKE MY NEW COSY HOUSECOAT, FOO-FOO?

WALTER, PRINCE OF THE SOFTIES

HIS SOFTY DOG

Later—

YOU WOULDN'T WEAR THAT, WOULD YOU, GNASHER?

READER'S VOICE

NO—BUT I WILL USE IT AS A REAL "HOUSE" COAT! GNEE! GNEE!

THROW

B.B. can't stand it! A ball pinching bandit!

DOGGIE DEVICES

Bone Sausage Machine

All wrong—not strong!

THE NIBBLERS

What Whiskers says, each mouse obeys!

BILLY WHIZZ

Display dismay!